STUNT CREWS

Death-defying Feats

BROWN
BEAR
BOOKS

Published in 2011 by Brown Bear Books Limited

Copyright © Brown Bear Books Limited

Brown Bear Books Limited
4877 N. Circulo Bujia
Tucson, AZ 85718
USA
and
First Floor,
9–17 St. Albans Place
London
N1 0NX

Brown Bear Books Limited
Editor: Tim Cooke
Designer: Joanne Mitchell
Picture researcher: Clare Newman
Art director: Jeni Child
Editorial director: Lindsey Lowe
Production director: Alastair Gourlay
Children's publisher: Anne O'Daly

Library of Congress Cataloging-in-Publication Data available on request

ISBN: 978-1-936333-30-1

Printed in China

WEBSITES

The website addresses (URLs) included in this book were valid at the time of going to press. However, because of the nature of the internet, it is possible that some addresses may have changed, or sites may have changed or closed down since publication. While the author and publisher regret any inconvenience this may cause the readers, no responsibility for any such changes can be accepted by either the author or the publisher.

DISCLAIMER

The activities described in this book are highly dangerous and should not be copied or attempted by anyone other than a highly trained professional. The publisher is not liable for any injuries sustained while trying to imitate activities described in this book.

PICTURE ACKNOWLEDGMENTS

Front Cover: istockphoto

Interior: Corbis: Bettmann 16bl, Regis Bossu 10t, Peter Guttmann 28c, Hulton Deutsch Collection 9tr, Michael Orhs Archives 17tr, Reuters 12b, Robert Harding World Imagery 24bc, Andrew Winning/Reuters 29tr; **iStockphoto:** Anthony Brown 31, Lars Christensen 3, David Freud 5br, Rob Friedman 5tr, Matej Michelizza 24/25, Chritsophe Michot 5cr; **Photolibrary:** Martin Black 22cl, Key Color 6/7t, Goran Bogicevic 18/19; **Shutterstock:** Chip Pix 23tr, CIP Designs 16/17, Coral Coolahan 18bl, fdineo 25t, Hainault Photo 26tc, Hazan 27tr, Imagemakers 26/27, Joseph 4/5, Daniel Kryler 8/9, Mark Marketa 28/29, Reshavsky 12/13, RT Images 6tc, Tupingato 13t, Tony Wear 22/23; **The Kobal Collection:** Danjaq/EON/UE 20/21, MAM/EION 21tr; **Thinkstock:** 10/11, 14/15, 15r; **Topham:** 6/7b, 14b, The Granger Collection 19tr; **Wikimedia:** 8t.

CONTENTS

WHAT MAKES A DAREDEVIL?

Some people call them heroes. Others say they are crazy. But it's hard not to admire the bravery and skill of people who perform death-defying stunts. Do you have what it takes to jump over Niagara Falls?

SHOWING OFF!

Stunts are not for shy people. Showmen like Harry Houdini or Evel Knievel loved being the center of attention. They also had nerves of steel. Most stunts need good balance and a head for heights. Stunt people also need to be fit and flexible; they often practice gymnastics.

PRACTICE MAKES PERFECT

People who do stunts often say they enjoy testing their bodies. Many did tricks on snowboards, mountain bikes, or skateboards as kids. As they grew up, they learned different, harder skills. In fact, stunt performers never stop learning and practicing. This reduces the risk of getting hurt.

BEING FIRST

Daredevils often try to be the first to do something. In 2008, Yves Rossy became the first person to cross the English Channel using a jet pack. He whizzed across in minutes—but it had taken six years to develop his jet wing!

▷ **Top**: A stuntman wears a fireproof suit for a film stunt.
Middle: BASE jumpers launch themselves from a skyscraper.
Bottom: A motocross rider defies gravity.

◁ Even from a young age daredevils are always pushing themselves to do more dangerous, more difficult stunts.

THE HANDCUFF KING

Harry Houdini could wriggle out of anything: ropes and chains, handcuffs or straitjackets—even if he was hanging upside down. When other escape artists began to copy his tricks, Houdini went one better. He escaped from a locked case flooded with water!

ESCAPE ARTIST

The young Houdini turned to magic after seeing a magician. He started with card tricks, but they weren't very popular. One trick always went down well, however. Houdini swallowed dozens of needles and a piece of thread. When he coughed them back up, the needles were threaded together!

▽ *Houdini challenged policemen to handcuff him—but still escaped.*

DANGEROUS PURSUITS

Houdini realized that people got an extra thrill if he did something dangerous. In 1898, he started the "Challenge Act." He dared his audience to lock him up. They couldn't. He broke free from jail cells, padlocked crates thrown into rivers, and mailbags wrapped in chains. Soon Houdini was famous.

DROWNED IN APPLAUSE

In 1912, Houdini created his greatest act, the "Water Torture Cell." Houdini's feet were locked in stocks. He was lowered upside down into a glass tank of water. Curtains closed in front of the tank. A minute went by… two minutes. Silence. Assistants stood by with axes, ready to smash the glass. Three minutes passed. Was he drowning? Suddenly, Houdini burst through the curtains. The crowd cheered. How did he do it?

▽ *No matter how securely he was chained up, Houdini always managed to escape— but he never let the audience see how he did it.*

STUNT SKILLS

In 1909 Houdini revealed some of his tricks in a book. He had the ability to swallow lockpicks and keys and then cough them up at will. While he was being tied up, he gave himself room by holding his arms away from his body. Then he dislocated his shoulders to get them free! He could also hold his breath for over three minutes. This gave him time to pick the locks in the Water Torture Cell.

THE FALL GUYS

Daredevils have headed for Niagara Falls for over 150 years. On October 24, 1901, a 63-year-old schoolteacher named Annie Edson Taylor became the first person to go over the falls in a padded barrel. She survived the 175-foot (53-meter) plunge with just a few cuts and bruises!

△ *Annie Edson Taylor was the first Niagara daredevil.*

STUNT SKILLS

Annie Edson Taylor used a special barrel filled with padding. She tested it first by sending a cat over the falls! Others were less careful. In 1887, Stephen Peer tried to cross the river at night after a few drinks. He was found dead below the falls. In 1995, Robert Overacker rode over the falls on a jetski—and fell to his death. His special rocket-propelled parachute failed to open.

STUNT ANIMALS

In 1829, three local hotel owners came up with a stunt to attract more tourists to Niagara. They bought an old ship and sailed it over the thundering waterfall. To add to the drama, they put a buffalo, two bears, two raccoons, a dog, and a goose on board. The bears swam to safety and the goose flew off. But the other animals were swept to their death.

MORE DAREDEVILS

Later in the 19th century "The Great Blondin" crossed the river many times on a tightrope. He crossed blindfolded, pushing a wheelbarrow, or carrying his manager on his back.

The daredevils are still at it. On October 20, 2003, Kirk Raymond Jones leapt into the river and was swept over the falls. Seconds later, he appeared safely in the foaming pool below. He said he hoped the jump would make him famous.

△ *The Great Blondin once stopped halfway across the falls and cooked and ate an omelet.*

THE WIRE WALKER

▽ Petit walks the highwire in a town in Germany.

On August 7, 1974, Philippe Petit stepped on to an illegal highwire rigged between New York's Twin Towers, the world's tallest buildings at the time. He crossed between the towers eight times. He even bounced up and down on the wire!

HIGH IDEAS

The young Frenchman had learned to tightrope walk as a teenager. But he soon grew tired of ordinary tricks. He wanted to walk wires on famous buildings. First up was Notre Dame Cathedral in Paris, then Sydney Harbour Bridge in Australia.

THE TWIN TOWERS

Petit was obsessed with the Twin Towers. He studied the buildings for six years. He snuck in and studied the roofs. He hired a helicopter so he could take photographs and build a model to work out how to rig the wire.

SNEAKING IN

When everything was planned, the next challenge was smuggling the bulky gear past security. Using fake ID, Petit and his helpers pretended to be construction workers. On the night of August 6, they took the lift to the 104th floor, just below the roof. They rigged the wire between the towers, then hid until dawn. Just after six in the morning, Petit set off. The wind didn't knock him down. The wire held fast. And Petit walked into the history books … even though he was arrested by the police as soon as he finished his 45 minutes on the wire.

STUNT SKILLS

Petit's biggest challenge was rigging the 440-pound (200-kg) wire across the 140-foot (43-meter) gap between the towers. Petit and his crew used a bow and arrow to shoot a fishing line across the gap. They used the fishing line to pull a thicker rope across, then a thicker one, and so on. Last came the heavy cable. Other lines fixed the cable to the roof. They stopped it from swaying too much in the wind.

◁ *The Twin Towers of New York City were the world's tallest buildings until they were destroyed by terrorists in September 2001.*

NO STRINGS ATTACHED

Who needs ropes? Daredevils called "builderers" climb towering buildings armed with little more than a good pair of shoes. Alain "Spiderman" Robert and Dan "Skyscraperman" Goodwin have scaled buildings over 100 stories high.

UP IN THE CLOUDS

Imagine scurrying up the outside of a tall building without ropes or even a helmet. It's highly dangerous—and very exciting. At the top you might face howling winds, freezing temperatures, or swirling fog. Below, the crowd watches, open-mouthed. One slip and you'll be joining them on the sidewalk.

This sort of climbing takes many years of practice. Then it's time to get creative. Builderers clamber up almost anything: billboards, bridges, cranes, and chimneys.

RISKY BUSINESS

Such climbs are usually illegal, so many builderers head out at night. It's even more risky in the dark. In 2003, Tyler Miller bumped into a power line—and plunged to his death.

▷ *Alain "Spiderman" Robert climbs a skyscraper in Hong Kong in 2008.*

KNOW YOUR LIMITS

No wonder builderers need to be fit and fearless. But they're not as foolish as they look. Good climbers know their limits. That's how they stay alive. They say that it's good to be afraid. That way, you won't take risks.

Even the legendary builderer Alain "Spiderman" Robert finally gave up when he tried to climb the 350-foot (106-meter) Arche de la Defense in Paris. He had to be rescued by firefighters. Perhaps he had found the world's first unclimable building!

◁ *The Arche de la Defense is one of Paris' most distinctive buildings.*

STUNT SKILLS

Climbing up a building is like a puzzle. Many are made of smooth glass. It's hard to find grooves to use for hand holds. No special equipment is needed, however. Harry H. Gardiner, "the Human Fly," climbed more than 700 buildings in the 1900s wearing only his street clothes, tennis shoes, and a pair of glasses!

A QUICK GETAWAY

STUNT SKILLS

The runners go over walls, not around them. They slide down stair rails. They leap between rooftops, then somersault in mid-air as they land. They use park benches and parked cars like springboards. Welcome to the breath-taking world of parkour.

Traceurs combine the power of an athlete with the agility of a cat. But parkour is not about showing off or doing crazy stunts. It's not intended to be dangerous. You have to know your limits. Beginners are encouraged to learn the basics before trying more difficult moves.

ROUTE MASTER

Parkour is a French word meaning "route." The practice was created in Paris, France, in the 1990s by a teenager named David Belle. At first, this new activity spread mainly by videos on the Internet and it began to attract many enthusiasts.

In 2006 parkour suddenly became world famous thanks to the James Bond blockbuster *Casino Royale*. Belle's friend Sébastien Foucan was a stuntman on the film. In the opening scene, he did a series of incredible parkour stunts, including leaping from one crane to another.

▽ *Sébastien Foucan runs for his life in the James Bond movie* Casino Royale.

TRACEURS

Parkour is the art of making a getaway over tricky terrain—as if you're escaping from someone. Cat leaps, jumps, and commando rolls help you on your way. Runners are called traceurs. They "trace," or follow, the people who created the sport.

LIKE A CAT

Traceurs turn the local park into a gym. They bound up walls like stairs. They dive between fence rails. All the moves flow into one another. They look graceful and easy, but don't be fooled. Leaping around like this can be very dangerous. Just watching parkour is enough to get your heart racing.

△ *A mid-air somersault needs pinpoint accuracy to land and flow straight into another movement.*

15

CRASH! BANG! CRUNCH!

Stuntman Evel Knievel was famous for daredevil motorcycle jumps. But a mile-wide jump across the Snake River Canyon? Everyone thought he was mad. Even Evel wasn't sure he could do it. But he had given his word—so he was determined to try.

A LUCKY ESCAPE

On September 8, 1974, Knievel climbed into his rocket cycle at the edge of the canyon. With a roar, it blasted into the sky. The jump was a disaster. The rocket shot up so fast that Knievel passed out. Seconds later, the safety parachute opened. Strong winds blew the rocket back into the deep canyon. Landing in the river meant certain death. The crowd rushed forward to take a look. The rocket had landed on the river bank—just. Knievel had survived yet again.

▷ *Evel Knievel jumps a row of 15 cars in San Francisco in 1972. When he landed, he crashed and broke his ankle.*

CRASH LANDING

Evel Knievel often crash-landed, and the crowds loved it. He started out as a motorcycle stuntman hopping over mountain lions and boxes of rattlesnakes. The jumps got longer. Dressed in his red, white, and blue jumpsuit, Knievel zoomed up steep ramps and leapt over rows of cars and trucks. In 1968, Knievel was filmed as he performed a jump across the giant fountain at Caesar's Palace in Las Vegas. He crashed horribly—and became an instant star.

▷ *In his long career, Knievel held many records for motorcycle jumping—and for the number of bones he broke.*

STUNT SKILLS

Modern motocross riders do tricks just as spectacular as Evel Knievel, but they have much better motorcycles. They use ultra steep ramps to perform spectacular jumps. While flying through mid-air, they perform tricks such as backflips. Crashes are common, so riders wear "body armor" to protect their chest and legs.

PUTTING ON A SHOW

In 1975, Knievel jumped over 13 double-decker buses in London's Wembley Stadium. But as he hit the landing ramp, he flew over the handlebars. He bumped 65 feet (20 meters) along the track. Then his motorbike landed on top of him. Knievel had broken his pelvis. Despite the pain, he walked out of the stadium. The showman said, "I came in walking, I went out walking." In all, over his career Knievel broke 37 bones in his many crashes—a world record.

LOOPING THE LOOP

In the early 20th century, air shows drew crowds of up to 50,000 people. Amazed spectators watched as stunt flyers did death-defying loops and spins or walked along the wings in mid-air. Some even flew low enough to fly through farm barns.

BARNSTORMERS

These daring pilots were called "barnstormers." They advertised their show by flying low and dropping leaflets over a town. Then they paid a local farmer to use a field as a runway. Crowds would follow the planes to the field and watch the show. Some spectators also paid for a joy ride in a plane.

FLYING CIRCUSES

The pilots formed teams, or "flying circuses," each of which developed its own stunts. Jimmy Angel's Flying Circus

▷ Wing-walkers use struts to stay in place during loops and other stunts.

▷ *Lincoln Beachey flies under the bridge at Niagara Falls in about 1911.*

STUNT SKILLS

Charles Lindbergh, who became the first person to fly solo over the Atlantic Ocean in 1927, had once been a barnstormer. His favorite stunt was the "double jump." He leapt from an airplane wearing two parachutes attached to each other. When the first chute opened, he cut it off and dropped like a stone. At the last minute, he opened the second chute to break his fall. Crowds loved it!

hurtled toward the ground in a "death drop." Lincoln Beachey was the first pilot to fly upside down. Other flyers climbed from a speeding car to a low-flying plane using a ladder, or hung by their teeth below the aircraft. Gladys Ingle was famous for shooting arrows at a target while wing-walking. She also leapt from one plane to another in mid-air.

A RISKY BUSINESS

Many barnstormers became heroes, signing autographs for hundreds of adoring fans. Others made a fortune. But they risked everything to put on a show. In 1926, Bessie Coleman fell to her death when her plane flipped over in training, while Lincoln Beachey crashed into San Francisco harbor.

SPEEDBUMPS

No James Bond movie is complete without a nerve-shredding car chase. Cars race along twisting mountain roads or smash into each other. Although highly skilled drivers make some of these stunts look easy, they take weeks of careful planning.

AN AMAZING LEAP

In the movie *The Man With the Golden Gun* (1974), Bond is chased as he races toward a broken wooden bridge. With no way back, he speeds toward a jump ramp. The car twists through 360 degrees in mid-air and lands on all four wheels on the other side of the bridge. The incredible stunt was one of the first planned using computers. It was performed in one take, with eight cameras filming at the same time to make sure nothing got missed.

△ *Stuntmen often burn rubber to make stunts look as spectacular on film as they are in real life.*

▷ *Cars speed across the ice in* Die Another Day *(2002). Car firms let the Bond films use the latest models.*

FLIPPING MARVELLOUS!

In *Casino Royale* (2006), the stunt crew couldn't make Bond's car flip over. The ramp got bigger and bigger. Each time, the driver sped toward it at 80 miles per hour (130 kmh). The Aston Martin DBS took off—but it kept landing on all four wheels! The car was just too stable. The stunt crew had a trick up their sleeve. They built an air-powered cannon behind the driver's seat. It blew a cylinder into the road, flipping the car over. They did such a good job that the car rolled seven and a half times—a new world record!

STUNT SKILLS

On film, car stunts always seem slower. That means that, in real life, stunt drivers must go even faster. They might drive at 140 miles per hour (225 kmh), while a helicopter with a camera is flying just feet away. The cars are often expensive, so the driver has to pull off the stunt without damaging the vehicle. Knocks and bumps are all part of the job. It helps to be on the short side—you're less likely to hit your head on the roof during a stunt.

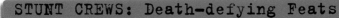
THRILLS ON FILM

Leaping from buildings; skiing off mountains; jumping from horse to horse; being thrown across a room in a fight; even being set on fire ... a movie stuntman can be asked to do virtually anything, as long as it's dangerous.

◁ *Being set on fire is one of the most dangerous—but most spectacular—stunts.*

OVER THE EDGE

In 1976, stuntman Rick Sylvester skied off Mount Asgard in Canada for the opening sequence of a James Bond film. There were no computer effects and no camera tricks. The stunt almost went wrong: a ski snagged on Rick's parachute as it opened. So how what does it take to be an action hero like Rick?

STUNT SKILLS

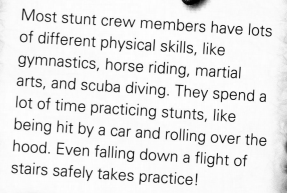

Most stunt crew members have lots of different physical skills, like gymnastics, horse riding, martial arts, and scuba diving. They spend a lot of time practicing stunts, like being hit by a car and rolling over the hood. Even falling down a flight of stairs safely takes practice!

▷ *Stunts are nothing new. This daredevil jumped between cliffs in the Grand Canyon for the camera in about 1900.*

LEARNING THE ROPES

Most beginners work with an experienced crew. They start with small stunts, like being punched in a fight. Big fight scenes take a lot of planning. Even fake weapons can be dangerous. The actor Brandon Lee was killed by a gun prop in 1993. So every move is thought out and practiced over and over again.

HARD KNOCKS

It's easy to get hurt falling down mountains or leaping onto or off horses. Stunt performers get bumps and bruises all the time. They take great risks in order to make movies look real. In some of the most dangerous scenes, people are set on fire. They wear fireproof clothes and gloves. A hood covers their hands and face. For large explosions, an air ram is used to blast the stunt performer across the set. Does this sound like the job for you?

ON THE REBOUND

Bungee jumpers dive from a great height. At the last moment, a cord around their ankles pulls them back into the air. They add to the thrill by jumping backward, or by jumping from balloons and helicopters!

FALLING OUT...

Bungee jumping started on Pentecost Island in the South Pacific. It commemorates a legend in which a wife escaped her cruel husband by diving out of a tree with a vine tied around her ankle.

In honor of the story, each year local people build a jumping tower on the side of a hill. Young men jump off the platform with vines tied to their ankles as a test of their courage.

In 1970, a reporter named Kal Muller became the first outsider to try this "land diving." He loved it. Word soon spread.

▷ *On Pentecost Island, many jumpers hit the ground, but it slopes steeply so they are not badly hurt.*

△ *New Zealander A.J. Hackett jumped from the Eiffel Tower.*

STUNT SKILLS

Extreme jumpers test their skills by trying to pick up an item off the ground. This is really dangerous because they get so close to the ground. Get it wrong and you'll hit the ground hard. Some jumpers use a colleague as a "sandbag." At the bottom of the jump, the jumper lets go of the other person, who lands in the water. But let go too early, and it's certain death.

BUNGEE SPREADS

Instead of using vines, jumpers used elastic ropes that stretched before yanking them back into the air. By the 1980s people were jumping from bridges everywhere. In 1987, a jumper even leapt off the Eiffel Tower in Paris.

SANDBAGGING

Hardcore bungee jumpers have found a way to make things more dangerous: "sandbagging." They carry a sandbag, which they drop at the bottom of the jump. The extra weight makes the rope stretch further, so they fly back up a lot higher and faster than normal. If they're lucky, they just miss the jumping platform!

SHORT, SHARP, SHOCK

There are extreme sports. Then there's BASE jumping. A tiny figure hurtles off the top of a tall tower and tumbles toward the ground at deadly speed. Your heart jumps. At the very last moment, a parachute opens. The figure floats safely to the ground. Phew!

STUNT SKILLS

BASE jumping sounds crazy, but it takes skill and practice. You need to carry out at least 200 regular skydives first. You have to pack your parachute well. If it fails, there is no time for a reserve chute to open. Getting into the right body position is also vital. Flying in the wrong direction leads to disaster if you're jumping off a cliff.

WHAT IS BASE JUMPING?

For BASE jumpers, leaping out of a plane isn't enough. They prefer jumping much closer to the ground. The word BASE comes from four locations for jumps: Building, Antenna, Span (bridges) and Earth (cliffs). Most jumps last less than two minutes, so jumpers use "ram air" parachutes that open fast. In 1990, Russell Powell jumped inside St. Paul's Cathedral in London, a drop of just 98 feet (30 metres)!

▷ *A BASE jumpers' view from the top of the Burj Khalifa, Dubai.*

▷ *Cliffs like those surrounding this fjord are a favorite location: they provide the "E" (for "Earth") in BASE jumping.*

LAW-BREAKERS!

Each BASE jump is unique. Leaping off a city skyscraper is very different from dropping off a waterfall. Some daredevils also jump from moving trains. Once the parachute is opened, jumpers steer away from hazards on the ground, such as roads or rivers— or waiting police! BASE jumping is illegal in many countries. Jumpers are seen as nuisances who endanger themselves and others.

In May 2008, two BASE jumpers dressed as building workers to sneak into Burj Khalifa, in Dubai, the tallest building in the world. They jumped off a balcony on the 158th floor.

27

TAKING THE PLUNGE

Watching cliff divers is enough to give anyone goosebumps. Divers stare death in the face before every dive. The sport isn't known as "tombstoning" for nothing. Can you imagine jumping off an eight-story building into the water?

A TEST OF COURAGE

High diving was once a test of courage for warriors. Kahekili was the last king of Maui, an island in Hawaii. In 1770, he leapt from Kaunolu, a 62-foot high (19-meter) cliff, and entered the water without a splash! The stunt earned him the nickname "Birdman." Later, he made his warriors jump from cliffs to prove their loyalty. They couldn't refuse: Kahekili was a 6.5-foot (2-meter) giant built like a tank!

△ *Divers at Acapulco make their dives as waves enter the inlet below—otherwise the water will be too shallow.*

ACAPULCO DIVERS

Today, cliff divers compete all over the world. Perhaps the most famous high diving site is La Quebrada, or "The Break," in Acapulco, Mexico. High diving started here as a dare between friends in 1934. The winner, Enrique Apac Rios, was just 13 years old when he made the first jump.

The cliffs are over 90 feet (27 meters) high, but height isn't the only danger. Divers must leap out to avoid the rocks below. The sea rushes in and out of a narrow canyon. Get your timing wrong, and you'll hit the bottom—possibly with fatal consequences.

▷ *The higher the dive, the more time there is to do somersaults and tricks.*

STUNT SKILLS

Sailing through the air at high speed is fun. The tricky bit is hitting the water at 45 miles per hour (75 kmh). At that speed, the water feels more like a brick wall than a bubble bath. The force could break bones or knock you out. Watch the experts. They do tucks, somersaults, and twists. But they always enter the water in a straight line. Landing in a flat "pancake" could kill you.

29

GLOSSARY

air ram a device that uses compressed air to catapult a stunt performer through the air.

barnstormer a nickname for stunt flyers in the 1920s.

builderer someone who climbs tall buildings and other structures without ropes or other safety equipment; also known as an urban climber.

bungee a highly elastic rope made of latex.

cable a very strong, thick rope made of twisted steel wire.

commando roll a somersault in which the weight on the body is placed on one shoulder to help cushion the impact of landing after a fall.

daredevil a reckless person or someone who makes a living by taking risks.

dislocate to move something out of its usual place, such as pushing a bone out of its joint.

escape artist someone who makes a living by escaping from handcuffs, straitjackets, cages, and other traps; also called an escapologist.

flying circus a team of barnstormers who performed stunts together.

jet wing a one-person, jet-powered flying machine; it is launched from a plane and the user must parachute down to the ground when the flight is over.

lockpick a tool for picking locks without needing the original key.

loop-the-loop a flying stunt in which the plane does a vertical circle in the sky, flying upside down at the top of the circle.

pancake a term used to describe landing flat on your belly or back after a dive; if done from a height this can be very dangerous.

parkour the sport of moving as quickly and efficiently as possible from one place to another using just your body, by climbing, jumping, and rolling.

ram air parachute a modern parachute that opens quickly and gives the jumper a lot of control and an extremely soft landing.

rigging any equipment that is needed when setting up a stunt, such as ropes, pulleys, and safety harnesses.

sandbagging carrying an extra weight, such as a sandbag, to make a bungee rope stretch even further.

stunt a difficult or dangerous feat, usually requiring a special skill.

tightrope a tightly stretched rope—usually a wire—on which acrobats perform high above the ground.

traceur someone who performs parkour, "tracing" the footsteps of the people who invented the sport.

trick riding horse riding stunts such as standing upright on a galloping horse.

wing walking an aerial stunt in which a person climbs on to the wing of a biplane while it flies, or flies while strapped in a frame on top of an aircraft.

wire walker another word for a tightrope walker or acrobat.

FURTHER READING

BOOKS

Armentrout, David, and Patricia Armentrout. *Stunts, Tricks, and Jumps* (Motorcycle Mania). Rourke Publishing, 2007.

Catel, Patrick. *Surviving Stunts and Other Amazing Feats* (Raintree Freestyle). Raintree, 2011.

Clemson, Wendy, and David Clemson. *Using Math to Create a Movie Stunt*. Gareth Stevens Publishing, 2004.

Dayton, Connor. *Tricks with Bikes* (Motorcycles: Made for Speed). PowerKids Press, 2007.

Gonzalez, Lissette. *Stunt Performers and Stunt Doubles*. PowerKids Press, 2007.

Harrison, Paul. *Gravity-Defying Stunt Spectaculars* (Fact Finders: Extreme Adventures). Capstone Press, 2010.

Horn, Geoffrey M. *Movie Stunts and Special Effects* (Making Movies) Gareth Stevens Publishing, 2006.

Hyland, Tony. *Stunt Performers* (Extreme Jobs). Smart Apple Media, 2007.

McCann, Jesse Leon. *Yikes! Scariest Stunts Ever* (Fear Factor), Scholastic, 2006.

Mello, Tara Baukus. *Stunt Driving*

(Race Car Legends). Chelsea House Publishers, 2007.

O'Shei, Tim. *The World's Most Dangerous Stunts* (World's Top Tens). Edge Books. 2006.

Rickard, Stephen. *Stunt Man* (321 Go!). Ransom Publishing, 2010.

Ridley, Frances, and Steve Truglia. *Stunt Pros*. Crabtree Publishing Co., 2009.

Robbins, Trina, and Ken Steacy. *Bessie Coleman: Daring Stunt Pilot*. Capstone Press, 2007.

Savage, Geoff. *Stunt Planes* (Wild Rides). Capstone High-Interest Books, 2003.

Turner, Cherie. *Stunt Performers: Life Before the Camera* (Extreme Careers). Rosen Publishing Groups, 2001.

Weintraub, Aileen. *Stunt Double* (Danger Is My Business). Children's Press, 2003.

WEBSITES

http://www.popcrunch.com/ dangerous-movie-stunts
A list of 13 dangerous stunts performed by actors.

http://www.evelknievel.com
Official web site of the motorcycle daredevil.

http://uk.askmen.com/top_10/ entertainment/top-10-crazy-movie-stunts_10.html
List of great movie stunts.

http://www.guardian.co.uk/ culture/2002/nov/22/artsfeatures6
A stuntman's guide to outstanding stunts in movie history.

http://www.niagarafrontier.com/ devil_frame.html
A list of attempts to jump over or walk across Niagara Falls.

http://www.parkour.com
A comprehensive guide to all aspects of parkour.

INDEX